YOUR KNOWLEDGE HAS VALUE

The "Lollapalooza" as a Guideline for Successfull Eventmanagement

Talisa Gassmann

Bibliographic information published by the German National Library:

The German National Library lists this publication in the National Bibliography; detailed bibliographic data are available on the Internet at http://dnb.dnb.de.

ISBN: 9783346576774
This book is also available as an ebook.

© GRIN Publishing GmbH
Nymphenburger Straße 86
80636 München

Print and binding: Books on Demand GmbH, Norderstedt, Germany
Printed on acid-free paper from responsible sources.

The present work has been carefully prepared. Nevertheless, authors and publishers do not incur liability for the correctness of information, notes, links and advice as well as any printing errors.

GRIN web shop: https://www.grin.com/document/1167308

Inland Norway University of Applied Sciences

Lollapalooza
- A music festival

1. Lollaplooza's event concept

The Lollapalooza festival which is annually held during July in Chicago's Grant Park, is one of the most popular festivals around the world (Nbcchicago, 2021). With an extraordinarily high number of 385,000 attendees (2021), it can be said that this spectator based event can be categorized as a mega event (Bauer, 2021). Additionally, the global participation of the outstanding numbers of visitors, international media attention as well as environmental-, socio-cultural- and ecomomic impacts characterize the category of mega events (Müller, 2015). In fact, that the festival is public for every person around the globe, it can be concluded that this event represents the category of public sector events. In order to gain a better understanding, the following table is listed, to sum up the categorization of the Lollapalooza.

Table 1: Lollapalooza's categorization

Content	Target group	Size	Host sector
Cultural event	Spectactor based	Mega event	Public sector event

Source: Own representation

It is primarily of importance to understand the concept behind every event. That is the reason why a closer look at Goldblatt's model of the five W's is taken now. This model is not primarily of relevance regarding theoretical aspects, "[e]vent management has [likewise] adopted them as their working fundamentals and deemed them the [event elements] (…) and (…) must be considered from the point of conceptualization, throughout the event and to its conclusion (Molina, 2007). The following representation simplifies Goldblatt's model.

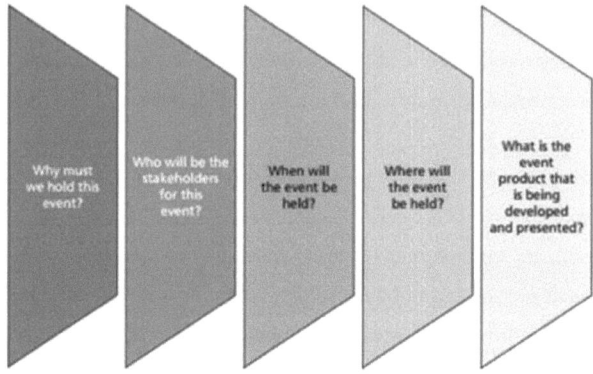

Source: Adapted from Goldberg, 2005, p.44

First of all, every organizer should be clear about the reason why the event must be held (Goldblatt, 2008). Music festivals have always played a major role in people's lives. Lollapalooza offers the unique experience to celebrate and get to know delightful heritage, traditions and cultures. The purpose is to celebrate special events and emotions in our lives with our loved ones and even strangers with whom we feel connected during a variety of magical moments. The festival also connects people in a special way by dancing, celebrating diverse milestones and sharing their background with other people who could be a new part of their lives. That is the reason why Lollapalooza reinforces cultural and social identity by strengthening ties within a completely newly created community. In addition to adding vitality to cities, the festival gives citizens renewed pride and could improve the city's image (Pavluković, Armenski, Alcántara-Pilar, 2018). It can be said that Lollapalooza adds a lot of glory to every individual no matter which gender, sexual orientation or race.

Another influential priority is getting to know the event's stakeholders (Goldblatt, 2008). Regarding the Lollapalooza, it is noteworthy that stakeholders can be divided into two categories: primary and secondary stakeholders. The classification of the primary stakeholders includes "(…) those on whom the festival is dependent [for example] (…) employees, volunteers, sponsors, suppliers, spectators, attendees and participants" (Andersson, Getz, 2008). The second category involves factors such as the government, businesses, the host community, tourist organizations, media and essential services (Andersson, Getz, 2008). Without those relevant groups of stakeholders, the Lollapalooza would fail in every way, as the stakeholder's interaction is fundamental.

Furthermore, it is equally important to clarify where the event will be held (Goldblatt, 2008). The musician as well as founder and organizer of "(…) the first reborn Lollapalooza in 2005 (…) [brought the festival to Chicago] to catch performances in iconic Gran[t] Park along the waterfront." (Neenan, n.d.) The "(…) festival (…) began as a touring event, [so] it makes only sense (…) to keep the tradition alive (Neenan, n.d.). As a result, Lollapalooza was continually expanded since 2011 and found new origins in South America followed by the spreading in Europe in 2015 (Lollapalooza, 2021; Neenan, n.d.).

As mentioned in the beginning, the Lollapalooza is annually held during the last days of July and has a duration of four days (Lollapalooza, 2021). But this time period corresponds only to the American festival.

The last step thematizes the final developed and presented product of the Lollapalooza festival (Goldblatt, 2008). The presented product is a crowd of various people from different nations, feeling the music from popular international artists. The interaction of every single person, regardless of whether the influence is directly visible (attendees, stage performers) or hidden at the first moment (volunteers who prepare everything, sponsors, people who are responsible for the technique, light effects, customs and food) are developing this unique product together.

2. Event experiences

Event industries rely heavily on the importance of experience, which ties into important variables such as loyalty or customer satisfaction. The experience is often viewed as the heart of an event and is therefore, a primary concern during planning and organizing events. That is the reason why they can be seen as stages and carriers for experiences. "Customer experience can be influenced not only by elements within the service provider's control (e.g., physical environment, service employees), but also by elements that are beyond [their] control (…) (e.g., the customer's previous experience, interactions with fellow customers, fluctuation in the customer's moods)" (Liu, Sparks, Coghlan, 2017, p. 463). For every event organizer, it is vital to create the most pleasant visitor experience which impacts the customer loyalty directly. In conventional events, physical presence is one of their defining characteristics which leads straightaway to a common and shared mood which the participants directly connect to the event. Resulting, the identification of process and behavior ranges transfer to the creation of social interactions like bonding, detaching, and belonging. Through this positive experience, the person will remember the moment forever, recommend the event to friends that they can participate as well and lastly, they want nothing more than to experience it again. (Richards, 2019; Lesić, Ružić, Brščić, 2017). "This type of consumer-to-consumer interaction (C2C) is increasingly important in supporting the atmosphere and ambiance of events" (Richards, 2019).

But how to create the optimal event experience? The answer is event experience design. The goal of event experience design is to develop a vision that "(…) guides event design and execution, and [conveys] your desired event narrative throughout the entire [event] journey" (Wong, 2018). By designing the event initially, the success can be guaranteed while understanding the audience's desires and needs. If these approaches are well thought out, it gives the event organizer the possibility to provide his target group a unique event experience (Wong, 2018).

It is impossible to design perfect experiences since they are also affected by factors such as social, cultural and personal. Nevertheless, Lollapalooza's designers should strive to create unforgettable experiences. The key to a guaranteed success would be the creation of immersion which is "[t]he feeling of being fully absorbed, surrendered to, or consumed by an activity, to the point of forgetting one's self and one's surroundings" (Mainemelis, 2001, p.557). Immersion is essential of importance because of the creation of positive associations while developing long-lasting memories (Vaccaro, 2020).

The first requirement that must be met is letting the festival attendees feel safe. The top priority is to carry out a proper bag check while entering the festival area as well as providing an exceedingly large security team. But the topic of risk management is discussed in more detail in the following chapter. To create the base of immersion the festival has to completely fulfill the visitor's expectation levels. In order to achieve this, it is vital to work continuously on it while conducting satisfaction surveys annually after the festival is over. While implementing this measurement the organizers let people involve so that they feel part of the team. Additionally, people's suggestions for improvement have to be implemented steadily. But, more important is to always bring new ideas that the audience did not expect. The creation of an overwhelming amazement can be achieved through the surprising appearance of live acts at the end of each day. If Lollapalooza's organizer knows that one of the audience's biggest wish is to watch a live performance of Billie Eilish but she was not announced in the line-up, it could definitely guarantee the most breath-holding and unforgettable moment if she suddenly performs. Another measure to meet the goal is to improve the entire atmosphere starting with the stage, ameliorate light effects and invent modern art installations. It will immediately catch the visitor's attention while taking impressively more pictures to share the moment with other people and to reminisce later on. In this regard, the organizer should also think about dimming the light during the acts to create a romantic and comfortable setting while handing out lightsticks for free.

3.1. Fundamental bases of risk management

An event's success is regularly measured by a variety of factors for instance through the economic benefit. By implementing risk assessment metrics and frameworks, a person can assess or measure the risk related to the object under investigation (Rogers, 2020). Yet, risk cannot ever be completely eliminated, even if it can be quantified and characterized qualitatively (Chapman & Ward, 2004). But to ensure the most successful event as possible, the level of safety is vital.

Firstly, it is primarily important to understand the relevance behind this concept. Pinto exemplifies this terminology as "the art and science of identifying, analysing, and responding to risk factors throughout the life of a project and in the best interests of its objectives" (Pinto, 2010, p. 221; Bladen, Kennell, Abson, Wilde, 2012, p. 25). Risk management takes place during the concept development as well as during planning, implementing and operating events (Chapman & Ward, 2004; Couillard, 1995; Tourism Western Australia, 2014). Eventually, the risk represents the uncertainty that an event has on the outcome (Tourism Western Australia, 2014). Uncertainty describes the unpredicted impact of problematic barriers which transfer mainly to the timing, resources and external factors (Bladen et al., 2012, p. 25).

Additionally, risks can be classified into four separate categories (Wilde, 2012, p. 26; Rogers, 2020):

1. Risks associated to technological performance
2. Risks linked to the project performance
3. Risks connected to organizational performance
4. Risks with regard to external performance

In production-driven organizations, the design team is irreplaceably dependent on the factor of creativity. The loss of key team members due to changes in staff, disagreements, resignations, illnesses or even the demise of a member affects important projects in a negative way. Such situations often don't simply involve replacing one person with another. (Wilde, 2012, p. 26). Thus, risk management is highly of relevance. But not only because of the previously listed losses, the concept is also needed to (Tourism Western Australia, 2014; Wilde, 2012, p. 26):

- Help throughout the entire planning process
- Minimizes unexpected costs
- Providing better event results
- Improved decision-making capability
- The participation of event attendees is dependent on how high the risk level is (Tourism Western Australia, 2014)

The risk management process can be identified as a five step action plan. The following representation illustrates this approach.

Illustration 2: Risk Management Process

Editor's note: This image was removed due to copyright reasons.

Source: https://www.360factors.com/wp-content/uploads/2020/04/img-five-steps-digital-risk-management-process-1.jpg

During the first step, it is paramount important to analyze what could happen during the event and how (Srinivas, 2019; Witte, 2021). The second stage involves data collection as a purpose to analyze potential risks (Srinivas, 2019). Next, the risks have to be ranked from the lowest to the highest harmful factor which has to be eliminated immediately (Srinivas, 2019; Witte, 2021). In step four you should "(…) evaluate the [available] options (…) to treat those risks and apply various methods and controls to achieve an acceptable [risk level]" (Witte, 2021). Lastly, results have to be steadily monitored and tracked "(…) to ensure that risks remain within the limits (…)" (Witte, 2021).

3.2. Risk management strategies for Lollapalooza

To avoid a tragedy how it happened at Travis Scott's Astroworls concert on the 5th of November 2021, it is essential that the Lollapalooza has a well-thought risk management strategy plan (Elassar, 2021). Since many risks can occur at a mega event, people's safety should be a top prioritity. That is the reason why alcohol and drug management, crowd management and fire safety have to be well-thought developed (Bladen et al, 2012, p. 130ff.).

Firstly, Lollapalooza's risk management team has to identify the key risk factors to develop a risk assessment. A successful risk assessment toll may allow safe future editions of the festival without harming any participants while reducing as many risks as possible. Potential risks that could occur during the festival are bad weather conditions, the uncontrolled alcohol consumption refers to losing control of people's behavior, crowds can cause a domino effect of panicking and crushing, the stage show including fireworks can cause uncontrollable fires or even explosions (Bladen et al., 2012; Park, 2020). In addition, it must be noted that the special effects and laser shows during the performance can cause damage to the eyes.

The next step is to evaluate the previously mentioned risk factors while using a table existing of the factors, how likely it can occur from rare to almost certain, the consequence consisting of the hazardous level from insignificant to catastrophic (Bladen et al., 2012; Park, 2020). The criteria for the respective consequence levels are illustrated in the following table.

Table 2: Consequence criteria

	Severity	
Catastrophe	5	May cause severe injury, disability or death, the complete loss of system, and major property or facility damage. May require immediate cessation of the event
Major	4	May cause injury or temporary disability. May result in extensive system failure. May incur significant financial loss and/or negative publicity
Moderate	3	Cause minor injury, illness, property damage, and noticeable financial costs. May result in minor system failure and/or negative publicity
Minor	2	May present less than minor injury or illness, negligible cost increases that can be absorbed by the project. If occurs, it can be controlled with a minor change to the event's schedule. May incur minor damage to the system as part of normal wear and tear
Insignificant	1	Hazards pose no threat to the safety or health of the audience or staff. If occurs, it may present no financial costs or no change to the event schedule

Source: Park, 2020

Additionally, the risk is calculated by the multiplication of the consequence and likelihood (Park, 2020; Bladen at al., 2020).

The last step in the table is to create strategies as a risk prevention and especially to take action if a risk factor occurs. Possible actions for bad weather conditions could be rain ponchos for free as well as multiple safety-covered areas with enough space for the festival participants if a thunderstorm occurs. Measures against uncontrollable alcohol consumption would be that every festival participant takes an alcohol test when entering the festival area to see if the person is still sane and can control his own behavior. In addition, it is not allowed to bring your own drinks and it would be worth considering to introduce stamp cards for alcoholic beverages, so that everyone who is legally allowed to consume alcohol may not consume more than a certain number. Actions to consider regarding a successful and safe crowd management is to definitely estimate the number of attendees in time as well as keeping the venue's capacity in mind (Bladen et al., 2012; Parks, 2020). "This forecast should be based on several factors: attendance in previous years, numbers who visit similar events, proposed level of publicity [and the] number of advanced ticket sales (...)" (Bladen et al., 2012, p. 132). But it is always recommended to allow space for much larger attendance numbers on the day. Another crowd safety implication for a safe future-oriented Lollapalooza is the installation of cameras to quickly analyze the crowd behavior and react as fast as possible. Lastly, instead of a large crowd where people can trigger a stampede at any time with the consequence of squeezing the front crowd, it is easy to develop a plan with several individual fields with a limited number of attendees. To ensure safe fireworks they have to be used with permissen of licensing authorities and under constant observation by a competent and educated person. The same actions apply to the usage of special effects and lasers. Furthermore, laser safety goggles will be laid out free of charge for everyone at the entrance to exclude all health risks.

In conclusion, the following table sums up the results of the Lollapalooza's risk assessment.

Table 3: Lollapalooza's risk assessment

Risk factor	Consequence	Likelihood	Risk	Measurements
Bad weather conditions: rain, injuries from hazards and thunderstorms	4	4	16	Free rain ponchos, Safe and covered areas
Misbehaviour because of alcohol overconsumption	3	4	12	Alcohol test while entering festival ground Stamp card for a maximum number of beverages (if they can legally drink) Bringing no drinks with you while entering Lollapalooza
Crowds panicking and crushing	5	3	15	Forecast Calculate space for more people than the amount of tickets that were sold Camera installation Multiple individual ground fields
Fireworks can lead to fires or even explosions	5	2	10	Permission of licensing authorities Professional and constant observation
Injuries caused by laser effects	4	2	8	Permission of licensing authorities Professional and constant observation Laser safety goggles

Source: Own representation

- 11 -

4. Lollapalooza's Legacy and Impacts

Legacy is a long-term impact created by an event that continues to be felt long after the event has ended (Bladen et al., 2012). They can be "(…) categorized into those that are economic, social, political, technological, environmental and legal" (Raj, Musgrave, 2009, p. 91). Sociocultural, political and psychological legacies, on the other hand, are much more subjective, so quantifying and measuring them precisely can be more challenging (Raj, Musgrave, 2009). Even though event organizers use the term 'legacy' in a way that excludes any possibility of a negative impact, the legacy of every event will have some impact regardless of the outcome (Cashman, 2005; Bladen et al., 2018). Additionally, Preuss has illuminated the interrelated aspect of tangible and intangible characteristics of legacy impacts (Bladen et al., 2012). The following table presents a summary of Preuss's series of impacts.

Table 4: Potential legacy impacts

Legacy impact	Tangible	Intangible
Positive	New infrastructure Urban realm improvements Increased tourism Urban regeneration Additional employment Inward investment and company relocation	Destination image/reputation Renewal in community spirit Increased regional cooperation Formation of popular memories Educational opportunities Production of new ideas and cultural forms
Negative	Debts from construction Debts from delivery Redundant infrastructure Increases in property costs	Opportunity costs Socially unjust displacements Unjust distribution or resources

Source: Preuss, 2007; Bladen et al., 2012

Positive Impacts of Lollapalooza

Substantially important is to mention that the economic impact of Lollapalooza remains significant. The festival "(…) created (…) 16,790 jobs and has resulted in over $1.692 billion in total economic impact" (Angelou, 2020; Daniels, 2021). Two years ago, 2,494 new jobs were generated in contrast to 2010 with 965 jobs. The highest growth is visible in the food and beverage sector, including 713 new job opportunities, followed by the retail sector with the creation of 356 jobs. The hotel industry is ranked on 3rd place (Angelou, 2020; Daniels, 2021). "Similarly, the largest sectors by economic output were food and beverage ($43.9. million), hotels ($31.8 million), and real estate ($12.4 million)" (Angelou, 2020). In addition, an amount of 7,5 million dollars were donated "(…) to the Chicago Park District (Daniels, 2021).
And even if it sounds contradictory, the event „(…) has [not only] a whopping (…) economic impact [of 140.000.000$] on the city of Chicago (…)", Lollapalooza is also

inevitable for the parks how "Bob O'Neil, president of Grant Park Conservancy (…)" has stated (Ponsce, 2015; OxfordEconomics, n.d.). Through ticket sale donations of three million dollars every year, it enables the possibility to create new gardens, plant several thousand trees and renovates gardens. For Mr. O'Neil and the residents is no doubt that the event improves the parks communitywide (Ponce, 2015).

But not only economic advantages become visible Lollapalooza also tries to achieve a leaderposition in eco-friendly and philanthrophy initiatives. The Lolla Cares is a program that was developed to bring international organizations together to discuss vital issues, such as volunteering, registering to vote, and saving lives. In 2019, a total number of 20 organizations were engaged (Angelou, 2020). Noticable highlights are summarized in the following table.

Table 3: Achievements

More votings	Bone Marrow Registry	HFTD[1]	Oxfam
Over 400	1,117 people added	220 new volunteers	3,025 more signatures for petitions

Source: Own representation based on Angelou, 2020

Lastly, "Lollapalooza Arts Education Fund, in partnership with Ingenuity (…)" was launched to "(…) invest $2.2 million (…)" for the support of "(…) arts education in [Chicago's public] schools." Investigations have proven that artistry programs have a noticeable beneficial influence on the academic-, social- and emotional development of a student (Daniels, 2021; Hayes, 2021). The fundings give the unique possibility to let students participate in trips, experienence performances and make investments in materials and items possible. But that is not the main reason behind the launch (Daniels, 2021; Masterson, 2021). Sadly, „(…) 35% of CPS students were enrolled at schools without consistent access to high-quality arts education" because of their economic situation and race (Daniels, 2021; Masterson, 2021). This project broadens the horizon for every individual student no matter if they are living in the middle class or not. To make everything fairer, a rating system was developed to prioritize the schools that needed the support the most. In the end, a total of 220 schools were noticed (Daniels, 2021; Hayes, 2021; Masterson, 2021).

Negative Impacts

Despite its numerous benefits, Lollapalooza has a variety of negative consequences, especially in the socio-cultural dimension. The image of the festival could gradually deteriorate because of behavioral aftereffects, caused by drug – and excessive alcohol consumption which can quickly lead to Déjà-vu's or in some cases even to an overdose. A growth in participants also increases the probability of more unintended pregnancies and STDs. Attendee behavior like this does not portray a positive light on the event. It could possibly damage the artist's image while news channels and social media follow every second throughout the days.

Chicago already experienced negative attention after a Covid break when the Lollapalooza came back in 2021. Even if they developed a hygiene concept, " [a] total of 203 people who attended Lollapalooza have (…) confirmed to health officials that they later tested positive for COVID-19, Chicago's top doctor said (…)" (Nbcchicago, 2021). The reason leads back to no social distancing, wearing no masks and PCR tests festival participants could take three days before the beginning of the festival (Nbcchicago, 2021).

Additionally, tourists who travel to Chicago to attend the festival can also negatively influence the prices in local restaurants, souvenir shops and other provincial operating stores related to the increase in visitors. Despite this, Chicago's residents pay the same price as the tourists, even if their circumstances make them less fortunate. This proves that the tourists and attendees do not simply transfer to a positive influx on the local community.

The environment is getting more important than ever before, therefore it is crucial to take a closer look at negative environmental impacts. The Lollapalooza and the festival attendees have a significant effect on the environment influenced by transportation throughout the festival time directly connected with carbon dioxide emissions, tons of plastic bottles, high fuel consumption and unbearable noise for residents (Larasti, 2019; Jones, 2014, p. 267). "Researchers [indicates] that Burning Man, a smaller festival than [Lollapalooza] generated 27,000 tons of CO2 from transportation, power generation, and art installations (…). If [Lollapalooza] participants release CO2 at the same rate, it would be approximately [135,000] tons over the [four day period as the festival welcomes five times as many people]." (LMU, 2019; Richter, 2019). Moreover, it has been determined that mega music festivals exceed an amount of 110 decibels which is enormously dangerous in fact that it significantly affects animal's behavior and influences the reproduction of precious ecosystems (LMU, 2019).

"Empty beer cups, water bottles (…) and napkins are some of the many pieces of trash found on the Lollapalooza grounds" (Polidori, 2019). In this regard, it is proven that a quarter of a million festival participants produce a total amount of 100,000 kilograms of waste during every single day and since more people attend Lollapalooza there is definitely no doubt that the number is shockingly higher (Sonberg 2019; Richter, 2019).

List of References

Andersson, T. D., & Getz, D. (2008). *Stakeholder Management Strategies of Festivals.* Tandfonline.com. Retrieved November 11, 2021, from https://www.tandfonline.com/doi/pdf/10.1080/15470140802323801#:~:text=%E2%8 0%9CPrimary%E2%80%9D%20stakeholders%20were%20defined%20as,%2C%20to urist%20organizations%2C%20and%20businesses.

Angelou, A. (2020, March 3). *Lollapalooza Remains a Force in Chicago Economy.* AngelouEconomics. Retrieved November 9, 2021, from https://angeloueconomics.com/keep-up-with-ae/lollapalooza-remains-a-force-in-chicago-economy/#:%7E:text=Since%202010%2C%20Lollapalooza%20has%20created,milli on%20in%202010%2C%20respectively).

Aulton, N. (n.d.). *Understanding event experience & behaviour.* Futurethinking.Fr. Retrieved November 11, 2021, from https://futurethinking.fr/wp-content/uploads/2015/05/Event-experience.pdf

Bauer, K. (2021, August 2). *Lollapalooza Had More Than 385,000 People, Officials Announce After Lightfoot Defended Holding Fest During Pandemic.* Block Club Chicago. Retrieved November 8, 2021, from https://blockclubchicago.org/2021/08/02/lollapalooza-had-more-than-385000-people-officials-announc e-after-lightfoot-defended-holding-fest-during-pandemic/

Bladen, C., Kennell, J., Wilde, N., & Abson, E. (2012). *Events Management.* Routledge.

Cashman, R. (2005). The bitter-sweet awakening. The legacy of the Sydney 2000 Olympic Games. Sydney· Walla Walla Press.

Chapman, C. & Ward, S., (2004) 'Why risk efficiency is a key aspect of best practice projects', *International Journal of Project Management* 22 (8), pp. 619–631

Couillard, J., (1995) 'The role of project risk in determining project management approach', *Project Management Journal*, 26, pp. 3–15.

Dailymail. (2021, April 28). *Burning Man festival canceled again due to COVID-19. . . after considering mandatory vaccines*. Dailymail.Co.Uk. Retrieved November 10, 2021, from https://www.dailymail.co.uk/tvshowbiz/article-9518081/Burning-Man-festival-cancelled-Covid-pandemic.html

Daniels, C. M. (2021, July 29). *Lollapalooza teams up with Ingenuity to donate $2.2 million to CPS*. Chicago Sun-Times. Retrieved November 8, 2021, from https://chicago.suntimes.com/2021/7/29/22598387/lollapalooza-chicago-public-schools-cps-donation-arts-funding

Elassar, A. C. (2021, November 8). *What happened at the Astroworld Festival: Witnesses describe scenes of chaos and tragedy*. CNN. Retrieved November 8, 2021, from https://edition.cnn.com/2021/11/07/us/astroworld-festival-what-happened/index.html

Hayes, K. (2021, July 29). *Lollapalooza partners with Ingenuity to donate $2.2 million to CPS*. FOX 32 Chicago. Retrieved November 8, 2021, from https://www.fox32chicago.com/news/lollapalooza-partners-with-ingenuity-to-donate-2-2-million-to-cps

HFTD. (n.d.). *Start the conversation*. Hftd.org. Retrieved November 11, 2021, from https://www.hftd.org/

Jones, M. (2014). *Sustainable Event Management: A Practical Guide by Meegan Jones*. Paperback (2nd edition) [E-book]. earthscan.

Larasti, A. K. (2019). Environmental Impacts Management of the Coachella Valley Music and Arts Festival. *Gadjah Mada Journal of Tourism Studies*, 2(2), 56-72.

Lesić, K. T., Ružić, K., & Brščić, M. D. (2017). *THE IMPORTANCE OF UNDERSTANDING EVENT EXPERIENCE*. Researchgate. Retrieved November 11, 2021, from https://www.researchgate.net/publication/321139924_THE_IMPORTANCE_OF_UN DERSTANDING_EVENT_EXPERIENCE?enrichId=rgreq-

Liu, W., Sparks, B., & Coghlan, A. (2017). *Event experiences through the lens of attendees*. Research-Repository.Griffith.Edu.Au. Retrieved November 9, 2021, from https://research-repository.griffith.edu.au/bitstream/handle/10072/364292/LiuPUB4311.pdf?sequence =1

LMU (2019, April 2). *Environmental Impacts of Coachella*. CURes Blog. Retrieved from https://curesblog.lmu.edu/environmental-impacts-of-coachella/, accessed on 12.10.2021.

Lollapalooza. (n.d.). *Lollapalooza is in 7 countries*. Global.Lollapalooza.Com. Retrieved November 8, 2021, from https://global.lollapalooza.com/

Masterson, M. (2021, August 1). *Lollapalooza Organizers Donating $2.2M to Expand Arts Education in CPS*. WTTW News. Retrieved November 9, 2021, from https://news.wttw.com/2021/07/29/lollapalooza-organizers-donating-22m-expand-arts-education-cps

Molina, N. (2007). *Developing a managerial plan to guide the planning process for charity events*. Digitalscholarship.Unlv.Edu. Retrieved November 9, 2021, from https://digitalscholarship.unlv.edu/cgi/viewcontent.cgi?article=1623&context=thesesd issertations

Müller, M. (2015). *What makes an event a mega-event? Definitions and sizes*. Zora.Uch.Ch. Retrieved November 9, 2021, from https://www.zora.uzh.ch/id/eprint/106250/1/106250.pdf

NBCChicago. (2021a, July 29). *Lollapalooza Begins in Chicago, and It Is Packed*. Retrieved November 9, 2021, from https://www.nbcchicago.com/news/local/lollapalooza-begins-in-chicago-and-it-is-packed/2571744/#:%7E:text=The%20four%2Dday%20music%20festival,

NBCChicago. (2021b, August 12). *203 Lollapalooza Attendees Later Tested Positive for COVID, Chicago's Top Doctor Says.* Retrieved November 10, 2021, from https://www.nbcchicago.com/news/local/203-confirmed-covid-cases-tied-to-lollapalooza-chicagos-top-doctor-says/2588834/

Mainemelis, C. (2001). When the muse takes it all: A model for the experience of timelessness in organization. Academy of Management Review, 26(4), 548–565

Neenan. (n.d.). *The Story Behind Lollapalooza, One of the World's Largest Music Festivals.* Www.Iexplore.Com. Retrieved November 9, 2021, from https://www.iexplore.com/experiences/festivals-events/lollapalooza-history-culture

Oxford Economics. (n.d.). *The Concerts and Live Entertainment Industry: A Significant Economic Engine.* Retrieved November 10, 2021, from https://www.oxfordeconomics.com/recent-releases/livemusic

Park, H. (2020). *Risk Management: The Case of Aspen Music Festival and School.* Lib.Dr.Iastate.Edu. Retrieved November 10, 2021, from https://lib.dr.iastate.edu/cgi/viewcontent.cgi?article=1004&context=materials

Pavluković, V. (2019). *The Impact of Music Festivals on Local Communities and Their Quality o.* LinkSpringer. Retrieved November 11, 2021, from https://link.springer.com/chapter/10.1007/978-3-319-91692-7_11?error=cookies_not_supported&code=1ef628da-dac1-4d3a-ade6-23138f5d8985

Pinto, J. K. (2010) Project Management, New Jersey: Pearson.

Polidori, K. (2019, August 2). *Lollapalooza increases green initiatives.* The Columbia Chronicle. Retrieved November 10, 2021, from https://columbiachronicle.com/lollapalooza-increases-green-initiatives

Ponce, A. (2015, July 29). *Lollapalooza Brings in Millions for City of Chicago.* NBC Chicago. Retrieved November 11, 2021, from https://www.nbcchicago.com/news/local/lollapalooza-brings-in-millions-for-city-of-chicago/108029/

Raj, R., & Musgrave, J. (2009). *Event Management and Sustainability*. CABI.

Richards, G. (2019). *Event Experience Research Directions*. Researchgate. https://www.researchgate.net/publication/336699933_Event_Experience_Research_D irections

Richter, F. (2019, April 18). *The Largest Music Festivals in the World*. Statista Infographics. Retrieved November 11, 2021, from https://www.statista.com/chart/17757/total-attendance-of-music-festivals/

Rogers, E. (2020, April 4). *Implications of risk management on project planning*. Linkedin.com. Retrieved November 11, 2021, from https://www.linkedin.com/pulse/implications-risk-management-project-planning-evelyn-rogers/

Sonberg, H. (2019, April 25). *Environmental cost of Coachella*. USD Student Media. Retrieved from https://uofsdmedia.com/environmental-cost-of-coachella/, accessed on 07.10.2021.

Srinivas, K. (2019, March 8). *Process of Risk Management*. ResearchGate. Retrieved November 10, 2021, from https://www.researchgate.net/publication/331783796_Process_of_Risk_Management

Tourism Western Australia. (n.d.). *An introduction to Risk Management for Event Holders*.www.cgg.wa.gov.au. Retrieved November 10, 2021, from https://www.cgg.wa.gov.au/Profiles/cgg/Assets/ClientData/Event_Resources/Tourism _WA_Risk_Management_for_Event_Holders.pdf

Vaccaro, S. (2020, September 13). *The Future of Events: Immersive Experiences*. Eventbrite US Blog. https://www.eventbrite.com/blog/immersive-experiences-events-ds00/

Wong, M. (2018, January 18). *Event Experience Design:The New Way to Craft Winning Attendee Experiences in 2018*. EventMB. Retrieved November 11, 2021, from https://www.eventmanagerblog.com/event-experience-design